From Columbus to the 21st Century

From Columbus to the 21st Century

A Brief
History
of Cuba

Editorial Capitán San Luis
Havana, Cuba, 2011

Translation: **Rose Ana Berbeo**
Editing: **Martha Pon**
Compilation and design: **Julio Cubría**
Sources consulted: **Instituto de Historia de Cuba**
and **Oficina Nacional de Estadísticas**
Original title in spanish: **De Colón al siglo XXI**

© On the present edition:
    Editorial Capitán San Luis, 2011

    ISBN: 978-959-211-357-2

Editorial Capitán San Luis.
Calle 38 no. 4717 entre 40 y 47, Kohly
Playa, Ciudad de La Habana, Cuba.
Email: direccion@ecsanluis.rem.cu

"A people is not independent once it has shaken off the chains of its masters; it begins to be once it has extirpated from its being the vices of vanquished slavery, and, for homeland and to live anew, rises up and gives form to concepts of life radically opposed to the customs of past servility, to the memories of weakness and adulation that despotic rule uses as elements of domination over the enslaved peoples".

José Martí

Índice

INTRODUCTION

Trying to cover the history of Cuba in just a few pages is not only a fanciful notion but a futile exercise. Our history is so rich that some periods have yet to be sufficiently explored, much less addressed with the objectivity that the passing of the years provides to specialists devoted to these matters.

With this brief look at the main events, divided into three periods — colonial, neocolonial and revolutionary — we shall attempt to familiarize our reader in a very general way with the long process of the formation of our nationality.

Here, too, you will find the main geographical characteristics of the island, its 14 provinces, and the special municipality of Isla de la Juventud.

FIRST INHABITANTS. COLUMBUS ARRIVES

When Christopher Columbus arrived in Cuba on October 27, 1492, and his ships sailed along the island's northeastern coast for forty days, he observed not only the enchantment of its lush flora and fauna but also the presence of peaceful, naïve inhabitants who offered him cotton, thread and small pieces of gold in exchange for trinkets.

Two years later while exploring Cuba's southern coast during his second voyage, the admiral noticed the diversity of those indigenous peoples, because the indigenous people from the eastern region who were accompanying him could not communicate with others from the western region.

The island first began to be populated four millennia earlier with the arrival of different migratory currents: the first probably came from the northern part of the American continent, through Florida, and later more came in successive waves, from the mouth of the

Orinoco River to the entire spectrum of the Antilles.

The approximately 100,000 indigenous people who lived on the island at the start of the Spanish conquest were comprised of groups with different levels of sociocultural development.

The oldest and most backwards — almost extinct in the 15th century — lived by fishing and gathering and they made their tools from the shells of large mollusks. Another group, without disregarding the shells, also used tools made of polished stone and in addition to their gathering activities, practiced hunting and fishing.

The more advanced groups from South America — from Arawak lineage — were farmers, and with their main crop, cassava or manioc, they made casabe, a food that not only could be eaten immediately but also stored. They made ceramic objects and vessels and used a variety of tools made from shells and polished stones.

For several centuries, their houses of wood and guano palm thatch, called bohios and grouped into small indigenous villages, were an essential element of the habitat of Cuba's peasantry.

COLONIAL SOCIETY

Spain's conquest of the island began almost two decades after Columbus's first voyage as part of the process of occupation that radiated out to different Caribbean lands.

Diego Velázquez, one of the richest colonizers of Hispaniola, was charged with bringing Cuba's territory under control and governance as a subject, and this began in 1510, in a long process of reconnaissance and conquest plagued with cruel incidents. Alerted to the abuses committed by the Spanish on neighboring islands, the indigenous peoples of eastern Cuba resisted the Spanish invasion, led by Yahatuey or Hatuey, a fugitive cacique from Hispaniola who in the end was captured and burned alive to teach the people a lesson.

With the founding of Nuestra Señora de la Asunción de Baracoa in 1512, the Spanish established seven villas with the goal of controlling the conquered territory — Bayamo (1513); la Santísima Trinidad, Sancti Spíritus, and San Cristóbal de La Habana (1514); Puerto Príncipe (1515) and finally, Santiago de Cuba (1515), designated as the seat of government. Basing themselves in these settlements — most of which changed from their original locations — the conquistadors began their exploitation of the island's resources.

Economic activity was sustained by the labor of the indigenous people, handed over to colonizers by the Spanish crown through what was called the «encomienda» system, a sort of personal, revocable and non-transferable grant via which the colonizer promised to clothe and feed these individuals and convert them into Christians in exchange for the right to make them work for the colonizer's benefit. The dominant economic activity during the colony's early years was mining, specifically for gold, an activity in which indigenous people were employed through the encomienda system, as well as black slaves, who, from very early on, were integrated into the ethnic conglomerate that would constitute the Cuban people centuries later.

The rapid exhaustion of gold-panning sites and the drastic decline in the population — including the Spaniards, who in large numbers were enlisted in successive expeditions to conquer the continent — resulted in ranching becoming Cuba's principal source of wealth. Due to the lack of gold, salted meat and skins became almost exclusively the goods with which the few colonizers on the island were able to enter the trade circuits of the nascent Spanish empire. Conceived under rigid mercantilist principles, the empire's trade operated like a closed monopoly, run by Seville's Casa de Contratación (House of Trade), and this soon awoke the jealous appetites of other European nations.

French, Dutch, and English corsairs and filibusters wreaked havoc on the Caribbean, capturing ships and plundering cities and settlements.

13

Henry Morgan

Cuba did not escape from these attacks: the names Jacques de Sores, Francis Drake and Henry Morgan kept the island's inhabitants on a war footing for more than a century. Wars and piracy also brought benefits. In order to safeguard its trade, Spain decided to organize large fleets that obligatorily had to make a port of call in Havana, strategically located by the origins of the Gulf Stream.

The periodic influx of merchants and travelers, as well as the resources allocated to financing the construction and defense of fortifications that adorned Havana Bay, such as the Castillo del Morro, became a major source of income for Cuba.

The inhabitants of more remote areas were excluded from these benefits and therefore resorted to lucrative smuggling activities with the same pirates and corsairs, who in this less aggressive way also evaded Seville's trade monopoly. Determined to eliminate this trade, the colonial authorities ended up clashing with local residents, chiefly in the villa of Bayamo, where a 1603 uprising provided early evidence of the difference in interests between the «people of the land» and the colonial government. One of the incidents caused by smuggling inspired the poem «Espejo de Paciencia» («Mirror of Patience»), the very first document in Cuban literary history.

In the early 17th century, the island — which at that time had about 30,000 inhabitants — had two governments: one in Havana and the other in Santiago de Cuba, although the capital was established in the first. Slowly, economic activity grew and became diversified with the development of tobacco farming and sugar cane production. Gradually, new towns were founded, almost all of them distant from the coasts. Primitive villas sprung up, where a more comfortable lifestyle began to be seen, with frequent leisure activities, from games and dances to bullfights and Altares de Cruz (May festivities). Religious activities, often the predominant feature of social life, left an important imprint on architecture, one example of which is the magnificent Santa Clara Convent.

The Bourbon dynasty's rise to the Spanish throne in the early 18th century brought a modernization of the mercantilist concepts that ruled colonial trade. Far from being weakened, the crown's monopoly was diversified and made itself felt in different ways in the economic life of its colonies. In Cuba's case, it led to the establishment of the tobacco levy, aimed at monopolizing, for the crown's benefit, the production and commerce of the aromatic leaf, which had become the island's most productive industry.

The measure was resisted by merchants and planters, leading to protests and uprisings, the third of which was violently repressed by executing eleven tobacco farmers in Santiago de

Las Vegas, a town near the capital. Unable to overcome the monopoly, the richest habaneros (residents of Havana) decided to participate in its benefits. Forming associations with merchants from mainland Spain, they were able to attract the king's interest and his blessing for the creation of the Real Compañía de Comercio de La Habana (1740), which for more than two decades monopolized Cuba's mercantile activities.

The 18th century was a time of successive wars between the chief European powers, and in terms of the Americas, they pursued a defined mercantile interest. All of them affected Cuba one way or the other, but without question, the most important was the Seven Years' War, during which Havana was occupied by an English expeditionary force. The Spanish authorities' ineffectiveness in protecting the city contrasted with the combative disposition of the criollos, the native-born Cubans, manifested above all in the figure of José Antonio Gómez, a valiant militia captain from the nearby village of Guanabacoa who died as a result of combat.

During the eleven months of English occupation — from August 1762 to July 1763 — Havana was a theater of intense mercantile activity that demonstrated the possibilities of the Cuban economy, which until then had been subjugated by the Spanish colonial system.

After Spain reestablished its dominion over the western part of the island, King Carlos III and his «enlightened» ministers adopted a series of measures to the benefit of the country's progress.

The first was to fortify its defenses, and the most important demonstration of this was the construction of the imposing and extremely costly fortress of San Carlos de La Cabaña in Havana. This was joi-  ned by numerous civilian buildings, such as the Palace of the Captain Generals (of government), and others for religious use, such as the Cathedral, which later became symbols of Havana's scenery.

The island's foreign trade grew, and domestic communication was improved, with the rise of new settlements such as Pinar del Rio and Jaruco. Other measures were aimed at updating government administration, particularly with the creation of the Intendancia (the seat of fiscal control) and the Administración de Rentas (tax collector's office).

It was in this context that the first census (1774) was carried out, which found a population of 171,620 in Cuba.

Another series of international events contributed to the island's prosperity. The first of these was the war for independence by the thirteen British colonies in North America, during which Spain, a participant in the conflict, permitted trade between Cuba and the rebellious colonists. The importance of this nearby market was seen a few years later during the wars of the French Revolution and the Napoleonic Empire, in which Spain also saw itself involved, to the serious detriment of its communication with its colonies.

In these circumstances, trade with the «neutrals» — the United States — was authorized, and the island's economy grew at a dizzying pace, bolstered by the favorable situation for sugar and coffee prices created by the slave revolution in neighboring Haiti. The criollo landowners became rich, and their new power was materialized in institutions like the Economic Society of Friends of the Country and the Royal Consulate, channels for influencing the colonial government.

 Led by Francisco de Arango y Parreño, these native-born magnates knew how to get the most out of the unstable political situation, and once the Bourbon dynasty was restored in 1814, they obtained important concessions such as free trade, the elimination of the tobacco levy, and the possibility of legally establishing their agricultural holdings.

But that significant material progress was based on a horrifying increase in slavery. Beginning in 1790, more slaves were brought to Cuba in just 30 years than in the preceding century and a half. With a population of over 1.5 million in 1841, the island was home to an extremely polarized society: along with the oli-

18

garchy of criollos landowners, the large Spanish merchants and the great mass of slaves, diverse middle layers subsisted, made up of free blacks and mulattos and poor whites in the countryside and the city. The latter were increasingly reluctant to do manual labor that was considered humiliating and suitable for slaves. Slavery was an important source of social instability, not just because of the frequent demonstrations of rebelliousness by slaves — both as individuals and in groups — but also because rejection of that institution led to pro-abolitionist conspiracies.

These include the one led by the free black José Antonio Aponte, quashed in Havana in 1812, and the well-known Ladder Conspiracy (1844), which was answered with brutal repression and which cost  the lives of numerous slaves and free blacks and whites, including the poet Gabriel de la Concepción Valdés, known as Plácido.

The colony's development accentuated the differences between its interests and those of the colonial power. Unequivocal manifestations of an emerging Cuban nationality, reflected in literature and other cultural expressions in the latter part of the 18th century, were followed by defined political tendencies that proposed dissimilar, conflicting solutions for the island's problems.

The cautious reformism advocated by Arango and other wealthy criollos was continued

José de la Luz y Caballero

in a similar, reformist-leaning liberalism embodied by José Antonio Saco, José de la Luz y Caballero, and other prestigious intellectuals associated with Cuba's large landowners.

Spain's rapacious, discriminatory colonial policies in Cuba after the loss of its possessions on the continent repeatedly thwarted reformists' expectations. This helped lead to the development of another political current, which pinned its hopes for solving Cuba's problems on annexation to the United States. This position was taken by a convergence of slave-owning landowners who saw Cuba's incorporation into the United States as way of ensuring the survival of slavery — given the support they would find among southern states — and individuals whose motivation was based on the possibilities offered by U.S. democracy compared to Spanish despotism. The first, grouped into the Club de La Habana, supported Washington's steps to buy the island, as well as the possibilities of a «liberating» invasion led by a U.S. general.

It was toward the latter objective that Narciso López, a Venezuelan-born general, channeled his efforts, becoming involved in pro-annexation conspiratorial activities after having served in the Spanish army for many years. López led two failed expeditions to Cuba, and after the second one he was captured and executed by colonial authorities in 1851.

Another more radical separatist current aspired to achieving Cuba's independence. This separatist movement appeared early on — the first pro-independence conspiracy, led by Román de la Luz, was discovered in 1810 — and reached a peak in the early 1820s. Under the influence of the continental independence struggles and Spain's three-year constitutional period, Masonic lodges and secret societies proliferated in Cuba. Two major conspiracies were quashed during this period: the Los Soles y Rayos de Bolívar (1823), with the participation of poet José María Heredia, the most outstanding figure of Cuban literary Romanticism, and later, the Gran Legión del Aguila Negra, encouraged from México.

Also during these years, the independence movement found its full ideological support in the works of the presbyter Félix Varela.

A philosophy professor at the Seminary of San Carlos in Havana, Varela was elected deputy to the Cortes in 1821 and had to flee Spain after the invasion of the «hundred thousands sons of St. Louis» restored absolutism. While living in the United States, Varela began publishing the newspaper El Habanero, devoted to spreading pro-independence ideas.

However, his efforts would not bear fruit for many years, because both the internal and external circumstances were not favorable to the Cuban independence movement.

In subsequent years, Cuba's economic situation underwent significant changes. Coffee production collapsed, demolished by Spain's clumsy tax policies, Brazilian competition and the higher profits to be had from sugar cane.

The sugar industry saw itself compelled to modernize production in the face of Europe's beet sugar initiative in the market. Increasingly dependent on a single product, sugar, and the U.S. market, Cuba was in need of profound socioeconomic transformation, but these were impeded by the major obstacles of slavery and Spanish colonial plunder.

The disaster of the Junta de Información, convened in 1867 by the Spanish government to review its colonial policies in Cuba, was a devastating blow to reformist hopes, which had been thwarted repeatedly. These circumstances boosted latent pro-independence sentiment among the most advanced layers of Cuban society, propitiating the articulation of a vast conspiratorial movement in the central and eastern regions.

STRUGGLES FOR NATIONAL INDEPENDENCE

The movement erupted on October 10, 1868, when Bayamo attorney Carlos Manuel de Céspedes, one of the principal conspirators, rose up in arms at his sugar mill, La Demajagua, proclaimed independence, and freed his slaves. The uprising, joined shortly afterward by the pro-independence conspirators of Camagüey and Las Villas, was able to assert itself despite Spain's ruthless reaction.

In the cities, Spaniards organized into militias sowed terror among Cuban families and became an influential factor in political decision-making, while in the countryside, the colonial army marched on Bayamo, the insurrectionary capital, which the Cubans were forced to abandon, but not without first reducing it to ashes as an expression of their unyielding revolutionary determination. Despite these difficult conditions, the independence movement was able to unify, and a constitution was passed in Guáimaro that gave rise to the Cuban Republic in Arms. The Cuban Liberation Army, after months of arduous military training, achieved an offensive capacity revealed during its invasion of the rich region of Guantánamo by General Máximo Gómez and the brilliant battles fought on the grasslands of Camagüey by cavalry forces under the command of Ignacio Agramonte. However, this military advan-ce was weighed down by political differences in the revolutionary camp, leading to the deposal of Céspedes from his office as president of the Republic (1873) and impeding the arrival of sorely needed weapons and resources from émigré patriots. An equally negative influence was the U.S. government's policy of hostility toward the Cuban revolutionaries; faced with the independence struggle, the United States preferred to adhere to its traditional stance, confident that Cuba's destiny would gravitate inevitably toward U.S. domination.

The Cuban military drive reached its peak between 1874 and 1875, first with the campaign of Máximo Gómez, marked by the victorious actions of La Sacra and Palo Seco and the Battle of Las Guásimas, when the Cuban Liberation Army defeated a Spanish force of more than 4,000 men, and then by the invasion of Las Villas by Mambí troops under the command of the brilliant Dominican general. But this extremely important strategic advance was once again weakened by internal dissent that hindered the arrival of vitally-needed reinforcements, leading to the invasion becoming bogged down without achieving its goal of taking the war to the island's rich western territories.

The weakening of the independence struggle coincided with Spain's recovery of its political/military capacity after the restoration of the monarchy put an end to the violent agitation that had characterized life on the peninsula following the «glorious revolution» of 1868 and the subsequent proclamation of the republic.

The inauspicious progress of the relationship of forces and exhaustion in the revolutionary camp caused an important sector of the independence movement to accept the proposals of Spanish General Arsenio Martínez Campos. The peace treaty without independence signed at Zanjón (1878) did not obtain a consensus from the Mambí forces, and was particularly rejected by General Antonio Maceo, commander of the forces in easternmost Cuba.

Despite his humble background, Maceo had risen to the highest ranks of the Liberation Army through his courageousness and combativeness. While revolutionary military actions could not be sustained for much longer, the Protest of Baraguá staged by Maceo and his troops and embodied in the most grassroots sectors of the revolutionary movement was the greatest evidence of the Cuban people's irrevocable determination to continue their fight for independence.

In the 1880s, the island went through a process of major economic and social changes. Slavery, already in decline as a result of the 1868 Revolution, was finally abolished by Spain in 1886. That was accompanied by significant transformations in the organization of sugar production, which was finally industrialized. Cuba's trade dependency on the United States became practically absolute, and U.S. capital was increasingly invested in diverse sectors of the Cuban economy.

The island's bourgeoisie, distant from pro-independence aspirations, was divided into two political formations. One was the Liberal Party, later called the Autonomous Liberal Party of Cuba, which had returned to the old tendency of obtaining reforms from the Spanish colonial system, including formulas for self-government. The other was the Constitutional Union Party, a reactionary expression of groups interested in Cuba's full integration with Spain. The independence movement, fortified in its grassroots base, drew its strength above all from Cuban émigrés. An initial outbreak, the so-called Little War (1879), once again led the Cuban people to the battlefield in the provinces of Oriente and Las Villas, but it was put down after a few months because of its poor organization and weak political unity. It was followed by periodic landings, conspiracies and uprisings, almost always led by the military commanders of the Ten Years War, and all of which were thwarted or crushed by the Spanish authorities because of their inability to join their actions together with a broad, united mass movement. That would be the accomplishment of José Martí.

Devoted since adolescence to the ideals of independence, José Martí y Pérez (Havana, 1853) suffered prison and exile during the Ten Years War. His ties with later conspiratorial movements enabled him to understand that the Cuban Revolution should be based on new programmatic and organizational foundations, a task to which he dedicated himself completely. Gifted with exquisite poetic sensitivity and brilliant oratory skills, Martí also possessed profound political thought, enriched by the experience of his years of living in Spain, the United States and various Latin American countries.

His work of clarification and unification, focused on Cuban émigré groups principally in the United States but with a broad repercussion on the island, crystallized in 1892 with the formation of the Cuban Revolutionary Party. Conceived as a single organization for all pro-independence Cubans, the party was to obtain the material and human resources needed for the new liberation effort, and to invest its military leaders with the political power essential for waging the Necessary War, which broke out on February 24, 1895.

Martí, who disembarked in Cuba accompanied by Máximo Gómez, commander of the Liberation Army, was killed in action soon afterward at Dos Ríos. Despite this irreparable loss, the Revolution unfolded in Oriente province, where Maceo — who had arrived as part of an expedition from Costa Rica — had assumed command of the Mambí forces, and it spread rapidly to Camagüey and Las Villas. In a meeting in Jimaguayú, the delegates of the Liberation Army drew up the Constitution that would govern the destiny of the Republic in Arms. The assembly elected as president a

27

patrician from Camagüey, Salvador Cisneros Betancourt, and designated Máximo Gómez and Antonio Maceo as General-in-Chief and Lieutenant General, respectively, of the Liberation Army. Soon after that, Maceo led an invasion column to Baraguá, and together with the forces under Gómez' command who were waiting in Las Villas, marched on western Cuba. After the victorious battles of Mal Tiempo, Coliseo and Calimete, the invading forces penetrated Havana province, provoking panic among the colonial authorities in the capital. With the arrival of Maceo's forces in Mantua, Cuba's westernmost town, the invasion successfully achieved its goal: the war had made its devastating effects felt all over the island, causing an abrupt decline in the country's principal industries. This time, Spain could not extract from Cuba the resources it needed to fight the independence movement.

To deal with the generalized insurrection, the colonial powers appointed Valeriano Weyler as Captain General of the island. He arrived in Cuba to carry out a war of extermination, armed with considerable resources. Despite the high human cost of this conflict — above all due to Weyler's rounding up of the rural population into concentration  camps in the cities — Weyler could not contain the rebellion; Gómez' campaign in Havana and Maceo's in Pinar del Rio kept the colonial army in check.

Although conditions were difficult, the Mambí forces somewhat periodically received war materiel sent by émigrés via the Cuban Revolutionary Party, and along with the weapons they took from the enemy, these enabled them to maintain their combat capacity.

In December 1896, Maceo was killed in action in the battle of San Pedro. Replacing him as Lieutenant General of the Liberation Army was Calixto García, another brilliant general from the Ten Years War. Gómez decided to concentrate on himself the best of the Spanish forces, subjecting them to a devastating campaign of attrition in the central region and leaving García free to wage important battles in Oriente and capture the fortified towns of Tunas and Guisa. In the meantime, thousands of medium-size and small skirmishes took place in the western region. The fate of the Spanish colonialism was sealed.

The development of the revolution in Cuba, seen with growing sympathy by the American people, led both houses of the U.S. Congress on April 19 to pass a joint resolution for the U.S. government to intervene in the conflict. According to the resolution, Cuba should be free and independent, and the United States would withdraw from the island as soon as there were guarantees of a stable government. Yielding in part to U.S. pressure, Spain granted autonomy to Cuba, a belated measure that did not produce the expected effect.

Then, in February 1898, the battleship Maine blew up in the port of Havana, and the event was used by Washington as a pretext for mobilizing public opinion and directly intervening in the war. Formally recognizing Cuba's independence without recognizing its institutions, the United States declared war on Spain, and with the collaboration of the Mambí forces, landed its troops on the southern coast of eastern Cuba. The battles were centered in Santiago de Cuba.

Blocked in the port of Santiago, the Spanish fleet attempted to leave and was annihilated by the superiority of the U.S. naval forces. After the U.S. and Cuban forces attacked the city's external defenses, the Spanish command decided to surrender. A symptomatic event: the Cuban military commanders led by Calixto García were excluded from the surrender ceremony and their forces were prohibited from entering the city. Months later, in accordance with the Treaty of Paris, Spain transferred Cuba to the United States without any consideration for the representative institutions of the Cuban people.

U.S. military occupation in Cuba

With the signing of the Treaty of Paris, the former colony's political situation became unclear. Cuba was no longer a colony, but at the same time, a republic was not being established. A transitional period began, mediated by the direct presence of the United States in controlling the island's destiny.

On January 1, 1899, the United States formally took possession of Cuba, thus materializing a longstanding ambition. It was now a question of defining Cuba's future, and whatever that was going to be, Washington believed it would be convenient for all of the Cuban liberation movement's representative institutions to disappear.

This was augmented by weaknesses and contradictions among the Cubans, especially disagreements between Máximo Gómez, General in Chief of the Liberation Army, and the Assembly of Representatives, the Revolution's highest political body, principally over Liberation Army discharge procedures.

31

The outcome was the disappearance of both institutions, which, together with the dissolution of the Cuban Revolutionary Party (PRC) by decision of its delegate, Tomás Estrada Palma, divided the pro-independence forces and left them leaderless.

The military occupation, legitimized by the Treaty of Paris on December 10, 1898, was the experimental framework for the implementation of policy on Cuba. For the United States, this was a time of heavy internal and external tension, affected by domestic pressures and negotiations related to government decision-making.

One of the factors influencing instability in Cuba was the management of the country's problems by groups that had their own interest, to one extent or another, in the outcome. Despite the efforts of pacifist groups in the United States, the pro-annexation tendency, in all of its variants, was gaining an increasingly important space in ruling circles. However, it should be noted that each type of pro-annexation stance featured a more or less pejorative concept of the supposed «infantilism» of the Cuban people. In other words, the baby, in beginning to take his first steps, could not be without the strong arm of his father to hold him up, help him, and protect him from possible falls.

One alternative obtained its maximum expression in the final months of the government of John Brooke, the island's first military governor, and consisted of transferring

Cuba's sovereignty to a civilian government that would transform Cuba, in a single blow, into U.S. territory. This idea gathered strength among expansionist circles and their principal spokesmen.

Domestic opposition to this proposal, but above all the Cuban people's rejection of it, led the new governor, Leonard Wood[1], to come up with the idea of «Americanizing» the island through a long occupation. This idea had two main aspects. The first was a broadly reformist project, with centralized control «from high up,» and in essence involved the transformation of Cuban society (schools, health system, legal system, government system, town hall, etc.). The second line of action was aimed at encouraging immigration, mostly that of Anglo-Saxon individuals, with a view to gradual colonization that would introduce the idiosyncrasies of U.S. society «from the bottom up.»

However, none of these projects had the purpose of transforming the former Spanish colony's outdated structures as part of a course to independence; instead, the idea was to create the conditions for promoting a «land market» that would facilitate the transfer of property to U.S. politicians, magnates and landowners.

1 Second military governor. Exercised authority over the island from December 20, 1899 to May 20, 1902.

Meanwhile, a lack of capital and sources of credit was placing the Cuban landed classes in an extremely disadvantageous position for reestablishing their businesses, above all those related to the important sugar industry, very much damaged by the war.

Nevertheless, the necessity of a change in policy was growing by the day, and as early as 1899, there was talk of the possibility of paving the way for annexation, not through prolonged direct military occupation, but by establishing a republic under certain conditions. The supposed inability of Cubans to govern themselves would very soon and very naturally lead them to ask their powerful neighbor for annexation.

The cornerstone would be to dictate the regulations regarding the convening of the Cuban Constituent Assembly under military law No. 301 of July 25, 1900, according to which the assembly was supposed to draft and pass a Cuban constitution, and as part of that, to stipulate, with the U.S. government's agreement, what kind of relations would exist between the two governments.

While the Cuban commission charged with reporting on future relations between Cuba and the United States was meeting, the U.S. Congress passed the Platt Amendment, whereby the U.S. government gave itself the right to intervene in Cuba's internal affairs whenever it considered it appropriate.

The United States had imposed an ultimatum on the Cuban people: either a republic with an amendment limiting their independence or continued occupation and despite opposition among the Constituent Assembly's delegates, U.S. pressure finally led them to pass the amendment as part of the Cuban Constitution on June 12, 1901.

First decades of the neocolonial republic

On May 20, 1902, the neocolonial republic was established. Its first president, Tomás Estrada Palma[2], relied on the approval of U.S. authorities as a potential check on the political rise of the more radical Cuban military leaders. At the same time, Estrada Palma's prestige within revolutionary circles  made him a favorite candidate among broad layers of the Cuban population. The existing lack of unity was accentuated by the disaster of the slate proposed by Máximo Gómez, with Estrada Palma for president and Bartolomé Masó, who had been the last

2 Tomás Estrada Palma (1835-1908). First president of the neocolonial republic. His decision to run for reelection in 1905 produced deep disquiet among his political rivals and different popular sectors. In face of his imminent defeat, he requested and obtained another U.S. military intervention in Cuba.

president of the Republic in Arms, as vice president.

This first government had the difficult, disagreeable, and thankless task of formalizing relations of dependency with the United States. To that effect, a number of treaties were signed. These included one on commercial reciprocity, ensuring the United States control over the Cuban market and consolidating the one-crop structure of the Cuban economy; the Permanent Treaty, which gave a legal framework to the Platt Amendment's stipulations, and a treaty defining the location of U.S. naval stations.

President Estrada Palma's characteristic austerity won him prestige for being honest, a reputation further strengthened by the brazenness of the presidents who followed him. On the other hand, the old president could not escape from his political ambitions, and he was reelected in rigged elections, beginning a tradition that remained unchanging in republican history.

This prompted an uprising by the opposition Liberal Party, setting off a chain of events that led to further U.S. intervention. For almost three years, from 1906 to 1909, the island was under U.S. administration, a period that contributed to defining the traits of the republican system, a strange combination of legal controls and government corruption.

Under the dominion of the Platt Amendment, political parties formed on the basis of local political bosses and patronage, and basically two parties — the Liberals and Conservatives

— struggled for power through election fraud and attempted uprisings.

The public treasury was the victor's spoils, a source of enrichment for a «political class» that, considering U.S. capital's growing control over the Cuban economy, could not find anywhere else to make better use of its talents. Thus, scandals often arose in relation to government administration.

These scandals abounded under the government of José Miguel Gómez (1909-1913)[3], whose mandate was marked, moreover, by its savage repression of the uprising of the Independents of Color, a movement of many blacks and mulattos who

were trying to fight racial discrimination, although without a clear awareness of how to do so.

The severe conservatism of Gómez's successor, Mario García Menocal (1913-1920)[4], was not enough

3 Major General José Miguel Gómez (1858-1921). Became president on January 28, 1909, as the second U.S. military occupation was ending. His government was characterized by a rise in political and administrative corruption and political crimes.

4 General Mario García Menocal Deop (1866-1941). Third president of the neocolonial republic, he symbolized the rise to power of the neocolonial oligarchy. He ended his mandate with a large personal fortune and

to hide numerous cases of corruption, benefiting in this case from the economic bonanza provided by World War I. Menocal got himself reelected through what were by then the usual procedures, sparking another rebellion by the Liberals and subsequent U.S. intervention.

Crisis of the neocolonial system

Washington, worried about the frequent political upheavals in its neocolony, had designed a policy of true tutelage — so-called preventive diplomacy. It reached its peak with  the appointment of General Enoch Crowder as a virtual proconsul to supervise and control the government of Alfredo Zayas (1921-1925)[5], under whose administration very important political movements would arise.

Generalized repudiation of U.S. interference and government corruption gave rise to diverse currents expressing nationalist and democratic demands.

The student movement demonstrated a marked radicalism; with university reform as its

---

in the process of becoming a large landowner.

5 Dr. Alfredo Zayas y Alfonso (1861-1934). Cuba's fourth president. His government was characterized by the open interference of the U.S. government and by a series of public scandals stemming from government measures and financial operations that affected the national treasury to the benefit of private foreign and domestic interests.

backbone, it quickly went beyond its original framework, taking on openly revolutionary projections under the leadership of Julio Antonio Mella.[6]

The labor movement, with roots that went back to the late 19th century, also had followed a rising course marked by strikes — the Apprentice Strike of 1902 and the Currency Strike of 1907 were among the most important — that later turned into a virtual wave due to the inflation resulting from World War I.

The proletariat's ideological and organizational advance, with its echoes of Russia's October Revolution, was concretized in the formation of a national workers' federation in 1925. At the same time, as an expression of the combination of the most radical political currents personified by Mella and Carlos Baliño, the first Communist Party was founded in Havana.

The political and social upheavals had very deep-going causes. The Cuban economy had grown very rapidly during the first two decades of the century, stimulated by commercial reci-

6 Julio Antonio Mella Mac Partland (1903-1929). One of the most outstanding figures of the Cuban revolutionary movement in the neocolonial republic. Founder of the Federation of University Students, the José Martí Popular University, the Anti-imperialist League and the Communist Party of Cuba. He was assassinated in Mexico on January 10, 1929 by agents of Gerardo Machado.

procity with the United States and the favorable juncture created by the recent world war. Nevertheless, that growth was extremely unilateral, based almost exclusively on sugar and trade relations with the United States. In addition, the chief beneficiaries of that growth were the U.S. capitalists who had flocked to the island at an escalating rate, given that they controlled seventy percent of sugar production as well as its infrastructure and collateral businesses.

The economic well-being derived from this process — evidenced by the sumptuous houses of El Vedado — was not only very unequally distributed but also extraordinarily fragile. That was seen in 1920, when an abrupt fall in sugar prices caused a banking crash that ruined Cuba's financial institutions. Shortly afterward, when national sugar production reached five million tons, it became evident that the markets were saturated, a clear indication that the Cuban economy could not continue growing exclusively on the basis of sugar. It was a choice

of stagnation or diversification of production, but the latter option was not possible because of the monopoly of land ownership and the island's dependency on the United States for trade.

Gerardo Machado's[7] rise

7 General Gerardo Machado Morales, president of the republic from 1925 to 1933.

41

to the presidency in 1925 represented an alternative for the oligarchy in face of the latent crisis. The new regime's economic program was an attempt to reconcile the interests of the bourgeoisie's different sectors and those of U.S. capital, and to assure stability for the middle layers and jobs for the working classes, all combined with selective but ferocious repression of political rivals and opposition movements.

Under an aura of administrative efficiency, the government attempted to put a stop to the struggles of the traditional parties by ensuring them enjoyment of the state budget via the formula of cooperativism. With the consensus that he achieved, Machado decided to reform the Constitution so that he could remain in power.

Despite the partial successes of its early years, the Machado dictatorship was unable to silence the dissent of excluded political figures, much less crush the grassroots movement. Beset by the regime's outrages and the rapid deterioration of the economy under the effects of the 1929 world crisis, these forces became increasingly belligerent. With students and the proletariat as its main pillars, the opposition movement waged an endless series of strikes, attempted uprisings, attacks and acts of sabotage.

The dictatorship responded with stepped-up repression, which reached intolerable levels. By 1933, Machado's teetering regime was on the verge of giving way to a revolution.

Alarmed by the Cuban situation, the newly-elected administration of Franklin D. Roosevelt appointed B. Sumner Welles as its ambassador in Havana. Its mission was to find a solution to the crisis within the traditional mechanisms of neocolonial domination. However, Welles' mediation was overtaken by events: on August 12, Machado fled the country, overthrown by a general strike.

A provisional government created by right-wing opposition groups under the auspices of the U.S. ambassador survived for just one month. An uprising of the working classes and soldiers, together with the University Student Directorate and other insurrectional groups, put a revolutionary government in power, led by Ramón Grau San Martín.

Principally on the initiative of Antonio Guiteras[8] as minister of the interior, the new government passed and implemented various measures benefiting the people. However, harassed by the United States and the opposition and to a great extent victim of its own internal contradictions, it remai-ned in power for just a few months. An essential

8 Antonio Guiteras Holmes (1906-1935). A leader of the revolutionary and anti-imperialist struggle during the 1930, he was murdered by the Mendieta-Caffery-Batista dictatorship on May 8 in El Morrillo, Matanzas as he was about to leave the country to prepare an armed expedition to bring against that government.

factor in the fall of this government was the former sergeant Fulgencio Batista, who overnight became colonel and chief of staff of the Army, and who negatively influenced the political process.

Restored to power, the oligarchic parties demonstrated their clear ineptitude for governing, despite the unlimited U.S. support given them through the annulment of the Platt Amendment and measures to stabilize the economy, mostly in the form of the sugar quota system and a new reciprocal trade treaty.

For this reason, the state's destiny was effectively governed by Batista and his soldiers, but this authoritarian regime showed itself incapable of providing a stable solution to Cuba's situation. That led to a transaction with the revolutionary and democratic forces weakened by internal divisions and was expressed in the 1940 Constitution. These new laws, which reflected important popular demands, opened up a new period of institutional legality.

The first government in this period was led by Fulgencio Batista, whose candidacy had been backed by a coalition of forces that included the Communists. This alliance, while producing important achievements for the labor movement, was not understood by other popular sectors, and became a historical factor in the division of revolutionary forces.

During the Batista government, the economic situation improved as a result of the outbreak of World War II. This situation brought even more benefits to Batista's successor, Ramón Grau San Martín, who was elected in 1944 thanks to nationalist and democratic measures passed during his first mandate.

Neither Grau nor Carlos Prío Socarrás (1948-1952) — both leaders of the Cuban Revolutionary Party (Authentic) — took advantage of the favorable economic conditions during their respective mandates. Timid and limited reformist measures passed by both of them barely  affected the agricultural property structures and trade dependency that were obstacles to the country's development. However, they did take advantage of the economic bonanza that came with the recovery of the sugar industry, plundering public funds to an unprecedented degree. Administrative corruption was complemented by the sponsorship of numerous criminal gangs, which the Authentics used to expel Communists from trade union leaderships in the middle of a propitious Cold War atmosphere. Opposition to the shameful situation that prevailed was channeled into the political/civic movement of the Orthodox Party, whose charismatic leader, Eduardo Chibás, committed suicide in 1951 in the midst of a heated controversy with government figures.

While all signs seemed to indicate an Orthodox victory in the 1952 elections, these hopes were crushed by a military coup. The discredit cast upon reformist platforms and the republic's institutions due to the experience of the Authentics, and the favorable attitude taken by U.S. interests and some layers of the Cuban bourgeoisie toward a «firm-handed» government, benefited the ambitions of Fulgencio Batista, who took power at the head of a military coup on March 10, 1952.

REVOLUTIONARY MOVEMENT 1953-1958

The inertia and inability of the bourgeois political parties to confront the military regime —some of them giving it their support — contrasted with the belligerence of the popular sectors, especially the young generation that had just come into political life.

Out of their ranks a new type of movement  emerged, led by Fidel Castro (Birán, 1926), a young lawyer whose earliest political activities were as a university student and in the ranks of the Orthodox Party. Advocating a new strategy of armed struggle against the dictatorship, Fidel Castro dedicated himself to silently and tenaciously preparing for that battle.

The action broke out on July 26, 1953, with simultaneous assaults on the Moncada garrison in Santiago de Cuba and the Carlos Manuel de

Céspedes garrison in Bayamo, conceived as triggers for a vast popular uprising.

After the operation failed, dozens of participants in the assault who were taken prisoner were murdered. Other survivors, including Fidel Castro, were tried and sentenced to severe prison terms. During their trial, the young revolutionary leader gave a brilliant self-defense speech, known as History Will Absolve Me, in which he argued for the people's right to rebel against the dictatorship and explained the causes, means, and objectives of the struggle under way. This speech became the Revolution's program.

Meanwhile, the dictatorship was dealing the critical juncture created by the drop in sugar prices by using the hackneyed formula of restricting production. To counteract its depressive effects, the government began a compulsive mobilization of financial resources that, to a considerable extent, ended up in the coffers of the regime's representatives. Despite the promotion of new lines of production during the two preceding decades, the Cuban economy remained under the yoke of sugar and did not attain satisfactory growth. The best evidence of that was the large mass of unemployed and underemployed workers; by the mid-1950s, they made up one-third of the country's workforce.

The dictatorship's attempt to legalize its status through spurious elections in 1954 served at least to placate its repressive brutality. The circumstance was used by the mass movement, which grew significantly in 1955, winning amnesty for political prisoners — including the Moncada combatants — and staging major labor strikes, above all in the sugar industry. That same year, Fidel Castro and his comrades founded the 26th of July Revolutionary Movement, and a year later, the Revolutionary Directorate was created, an organization of the most combative university students.

An improper promotion policy, the encouragement given to entrenched nepotism, favoritism, and brownnosing, and the lack of technical and professional training among some of the army's top leaders and officers were elements that influenced the decision by a group of educated officers to conspire to improve the institution's professionalism. These officers, called the «Puros» (pure ones), were mostly located in the Columbia military barracks, the La Cabaña fortress and in military schools. They included José Ramón Fernández, José Orihuela, Enrique Borbonet, Ramón Barquín, and Manuel Varela Castro, among others. After being informed on them, all of the conspirators were arrested and their seditious plan aborted.

Another event that worried the Batista regime was the assault on the Domingo Goicuría barracks on April 29, 1956. About fifty men attacked at noon and tried to occupy the garrison. Most of the combatants were members of the Authentic Organization (OA), led by Reinold García. The action ended in a resounding defeat because the men were expected, which was evident by the outcome: seventeen of the attackers were killed and none wounded, while the army suffered no casualties. The assault on this garrison, the base of the Rural Guard's Fourth Regiment in Matanzas, was an element that prompted the regime's intelligence agencies and organs of repression to act more energetically, especially to dismantle, neutralize and not underestimate groups of conspirators who were affiliated with the Authentics.

After demonstrating the impossibility of any legal struggle against the dictatorship, Fidel Castro left for Mexico with the goal of organizing an expedition of liberation forces and starting a revolutionary war. For their part, the bourgeois opposition parties tested out a new, conciliatory maneuver with Batista, in hopes of finding a «political» solution to the situation. Their failure ended up sinking them into discredit.

On December 2, 1956, with Fidel Castro in the lead, the Granma[9] yacht expedition  landed in Las Coloradas, Oriente province.

Two days earlier, underground combatants of the 26th of July Movement under the command of Frank País had carried out an

---

9 The landing of the expeditionary force aboard the Granma yacht on December 2, 1956 was the start of the guerrilla war in the mountains.

uprising in Santiago de Cuba to support the landing.

Because the two actions did not coincide, the uprising was a failure. After a setback in a place called Alegría de Pío, which scattered the members of the expedition, Fidel Castro and a handful of combatants were able to establish themselves in the Sierra Maestra Mountains to form the first nucleus of the Rebel Army.

Its calling card would be the occupation one month later of a small military barracks, La Plata, in an action that would serve to refute the dictatorship's claims that the expeditionaries had been completely wiped out.

In 1957, while the Rebel Army was flourishing in the mountains with a series of actions — the Battle of El Uvero being one of the most important — the underground struggle was developing in the cities with great impetus. On March 13 of that year, a Revolutionary Directorate detachment attacked the Presidential Pa-

lace in Havana with the goal of executing the dictator, but failed. José Antonio Echeverría, president of the Federation of University Students, was killed in this action. The dictatorship responded to attacks and

acts of sabotage by torturing prisoners more savagely and carrying out a wave of crimes. In July, the murder of Frank País sparked a spontaneous strike that paralyzed a large part of the nation. Soon after, in September, an uprising at the naval post in the city of Cienfuegos was evidence of deep cracks in Batista's armed forces. At the end of the year, the army failed in its offensive against the rebels in the Sierra Maestra, where two guerrilla columns had already become consolidated.

In early 1958, the revolutionary movement decided to accelerate the dictatorship's fall with an insurrectional general strike.

In the Sierra Maestra, Fidel Castro created two  new columns under the command of Raúl Castro and Juan Almeida, respectively, which were to open up two guerrilla fronts in other mountain regions of Oriente.

The strike called for April 9th came to nothing, with serious losses for the revolutionary forces. Batista believe it was the moment for annihilating the rebellion, and in the summer, he launched an offensive of 10,000 men to attack the Sierra Maestra.

In ferocious battles and combat — Santo Domingo, El Jigüe, Vegas de Jibacoa, and others — the rebel troops defeated the dictatorship's battalions that managed to enter the mountains, forcing them to retreat.

That was the definitive turning point. The parties of the bourgeois opposition, which until then had maneuvered to capitalize on the popular rebellion, rushed to recognize Fidel Castro's indisputable leadership.

Rebel columns headed for different points of the country, including the forces under

commanders Ernesto Che Guevara and Camilo Cienfuegos, who marched on
Las Villas province. Different
groups of combatants
were operating in that
area, including those
under the Revolutio-
nary Directorate and

the Popular Socialist Party (Communist). On
November 20, the rebel troops' commander
in chief, Fidel Castro, personally led the Battle
of Guisa, which marked the beginning of the
final revolutionary offensive.

In coordinated actions, the now-large columns of the Second and Third Eastern Front
began taking over surrounding towns as they
closed in on Santiago de Cuba. In Las Villas,
Che Guevara occupied one town after another
along the Central Highway and assaulted the
city of Santa Clara, the provincial capital, and
Camilo Cienfuegos took over the military barracks of the city of Yaguajay after hard-fought
combat.

On January 1, 1959, Batista fled the country. In a last-minute maneuver with the blessing of the U.S. embassy, General Eulogio Cantillo tried to create a civilian/military junta. Fidel Castro ordered the Santiago de Cuba garrison to surrender and called on the people to carry out a general strike. With massive support throughout the country, it ensured the victory of the Revolution.

THE EARLY YEARS

As soon as it was installed, the revolutionary government began dismantling the neocolonial political system. The organs of repression were dissolved and for the first time in many years, citizens were guaranteed the full exercise of their rights. The public administration was cleaned up and ill-gotten assets were confiscated. Thus, that terrible practice of republican life was eradicated. The Batista dictatorship's war criminals were tried and punished, the corrupt leadership of the workers' movement was swept away, and the political parties that had served the regime were dissolved.

The appointment of Commander in Chief Fidel Castro as prime minister in February heightened the pace of measures taken for the people's benefit. Rents were slashed across the board, formerly private beaches were made accessible to the people for their enjoyment, and companies that monopolized public services were nationalized.

One extremely important milestone in this process was the Agrarian Reform Law[10] passed on May 17, which eliminated large landholdings by nationalizing all properties  of more than 420 hectares, and granting land titles to tens of thousands of peasants, tenant farmers and squatters.

This measure, which eliminated one of the main pillars of neocolonial domination, provoked an angry response from the interests affected. The U.S. government had not hidden its unhappiness over the victory of the Revolution, and, after carrying out a malicious media campaign, adopted a policy of systematically harassing Cuba, encouraging and supporting counterrevolutionary movements with the goal of destabilizing the country.

The obstacles placed by President Manuel Urrutia to revolutionary transformations caused Fidel Castro to resign from office in July, but he returned days later in the midst of massive demonstrations of support, which determined the president's resignation and his replacement by Osvaldo Dorticós. In October, a military insurrection was quashed in Camagüey. It had been orchestrated by the military leader of that town, Commander Hubert Matos, in open conspiracy with large landowners and other

10   The Moncada program began to be fulfilled: the peasants were now the owners of their lands.

55

local counterrevolutionary elements. Meanwhile, the growing acts of sabotage and terrorism began to claim innocent victims.

In order to confront this counterrevolutionary wave, the National Revolutionary Militias and the Committees for the Defense of the Revolution were created. Together with the Federation of Cuban Women, the Association of Rebel Youth and other organizations formed later, they facilitated broader participation by the people in defending the Revolution. The unceasing U.S. hostility was materialized in successive measures aimed at destabilizing the Cuban economy and isolating the country from the rest of the international community. The Revolution responded with a dynamic foreign policy that increased its relations, and established agreements with other countries — including socialist ones — as proof of its firm determination to break its traditional trade dependency. In July 1960, after learning that Washington had cut off Cuba's sugar quota, Fidel Castro announced the nationalization of all U.S. property on the island. This measure was followed, a few months later, by the decision to nationalize the companies of the Cuban bourgeoisie, which, clearly aligned with the United States and oligarchic circles, had given itself over to systematic maneuvers of undercapitalization and economic sabotage.

But the U.S. aggression was not limited to the economic sphere. As the Eisenhower administration — which had broken off relations with Cuba in January 1961 — incited the creation of counterrevolutionary organizations and bands of insurgents in different parts of Cuba and supplied them with weapons and other resources, it also began to prepare a mercenary brigade with the goal of invading the island.

The invasion took place on April 17 in the area of Playa Girón[11], after a surprise bombing attack on Cuba's air bases. At the funeral for the victims of that attack, Fidel Castro proclaimed the socialist character of the Revolution, something that was being perceived already based on the measures taken in late 1960.

In less than 72 hours, the people crushed the mercenary brigade that had been trained for months by the U.S. Central Intelligence Agency (CIA). Despite this historic defeat, the United States did not relent in its goal of destroying the Cuban Revolution.

Under Operation Mongoose, a series of maneuvers of aggression were prepared that did not rule out direct military intervention.

That led to a serious international crisis in October 1962, when it was learned that Soviet missiles had been installed on the island. The promises via which the crisis was solved did not end imperialism's aggressive practices.

11   Girón, imperialism's first great defeat in the Americas.

Likewise, the determined action of our people, organized into the National Revolutionary Militias and Armed Forces, confronted the counterrevolutionary armed bands. Banditry was finally wiped out in 1965, when the last organized gang operating in the country, under Juan Alberto Martínez Andrades, was captured on July 4. Other dispersed bandits who tried to flee revolutionary justice were captured in the following months. That was how an end was put to a dirty war imposed on the Cuban people by imperialism and the reactionary classes, an armed confrontation that lasted almost six years and affected every province in the country.

In this dirty war imposed by the United States from 1959 to 1965, a total of 299 bands with a total of 3,995 members were operating throughout the country. A total of 549 people lost their lives and many others were left disabled, including combatants from the regular troops and the militias who participated in the anti-bandit operations and victims of the counterrevolutionaries' crimes. The country had to spend about one billion pesos during that time, which were difficult years for the national economy.

A combination of military actions with those of a political and ideological nature played a decisive role in defeating the bandits. The defeat of banditry in Cuba showed it was impossible to obtain victory in guerrilla warfare against an armed people that is leading a Revolution.

In the international sphere, the United States

was able to separate Cuba from the Organization of American States (OAS), and most Latin American nations — with the honorable exception of Mexico — broke off relations with Cuba. Nevertheless, the Cuban Revolution strengthened its ties with the socialist camp and Third World countries, participated in the formation of the Non-Aligned Movement, and developed an active policy of solidarity with and support for national liberation movements.

This nation, which determinedly resisted every type of armed aggression, also had to survive an ironfisted economic siege. The United States cut off all trade with the island and was trying to get other nations to join in its criminal blockade. Cuba thus saw itself deprived of vital supplies for agriculture and industry. However, the active solidarity of the Soviet Union and other socialist countries, together with the tenacious work and inventive efforts of the people, not only kept the national economy running, but also enabled it to grow.

In the midst of significant economic difficulties, unemployment was eliminated and

it was ensured that the population's basic needs were met. A vast literacy campaign in 1961[12] wiped out the old blight of illiteracy.

12   On December 22, 1961, Cuban declared itself a territory free of illiteracy.

Despite an exodus of professionals and technicians encouraged by the United States and particularly significant in the health field, the creation of a rural medical service made it possible to provide medical care in the most remote parts of Cuba.

For the first time, too, the education system also attained completely national coverage, and an extensive scholarship program made it possible for middle and higher education to be within reach of the entire population.

Quality of life improved thanks to a far-reaching effort to spread culture, which was materialized in the regular and generally massive printing of literary works, the creation and sustenance of many artistic ensembles, the promotion of the amateur movement, and substantial film production and exhibition. In the same sense, the generalization of the practice of sports had its influence, maintaining the growing and outstanding participation of Cuban athletes in international sports competitions.

This very considerable popular effort would not have come to fruition without the appropriate political leadership. Beginning in the first year of the Revolution, an integration process began among the grassroots members and leaders of the revolutionary organizations, but it was not exempt from difficulties. In March 1962, shortly after Fidel Castro denounced the existence of sectarian deformations in the process of creating the revolutionary organizations, the construction began of what would become the United Party of the Socialist Revolution. This took as its founding principle the selection of its membership based on their exemplariness as workers, elected within their workplaces. A decisive milestone in the materialization of unity was the constitution of the Central Committee of the Communist Party of Cuba in 1965 as the highest body of the Revolution's leadership.

By 1963, an economic development strategy had been adopted that, taking into account the Cuban economy's characteristics and prospects for trade with the USSR and other socialist countries, revolved around agriculture. A proposal was made to produce ten million tons of sugar for 1970. This was unquestionably a formidable challenge when considering the country's organizational, technical, and material conditions. In confronting this challenge, distortions occurred. The failure of the «ten million ton harvest» gave way to a revision of that policy.

INSTITUTIONALIZATION OF THE COUNTRY. WAR OF THE ENTIRE PEOPLE.

Beginning in 1971, the revolutionary organizations were revitalized and the institutionalization of the country began. As the culmination of a profound reorganization, the Communist Party of Cuba held its first congress, after having submitted its principle documents to a broad popular discussion. On February 24, 1976, a new Constitution was proclaimed after it was passed in a plebiscite, a direct vote by secret ballot in which 95.7 percent of the population over eighteen years old participated. The various levels of the People's Power authorities were created via a process that had as its basis the election of district delegates, nominated by citizens in public meetings according to their place of residence. During these years, the consolidation of Cuba's international position was also appreciable. The reestablishment of diplomatic relations with Peru, Panama, Chile and other Latin American countries broke through the barrier erected by the United States in the previous decade. After signing trade agreements with the Soviet Union — whose favorable terms of exchange were distant from the unequal practices of the international market — Cuba joined the Council for Mutual Economic Aid (Comecon).

In 1976, Cuban troops sent to Africa on the request of the Angolan government contributed to liberating that country from South African intervention. Shortly after that, another Cuban contingent participated in the defense of Ethiopia in face of Somali aggression.

The fact that the sixth Non-Aligned Summit was held in Havana in 1979 demonstrated the prestige won by the Revolution.

After a brief period of goodwill during the initial years of President James Carter's government, Cuba-U.S. relations deteriorated with the stepped-up aggressiveness of U.S. policy at the end of the same administration.

With Ronald Reagan's rise to the presidency of the United States, actions against the Revolution were increased to the maximum. The U.S. government created the ill-named Radio Martí and TV Martí, intensified its espionage against the island, carried out military maneuvers, flew test air raids, and tried to have sanctions placed against Cuba in the UN Human Rights Commission. The possibility of direct aggression had been raised.

Cuba responded by perfecting its system of national defense and creating the doctrine of «The War of the Entire People.»

Its essence was that each Cuban had a place, a way and a means in the fight against possible imperialist aggression. The preparation of the people in the Territorial Troop Militias, the Production and Defense Brigades and the Zones of Defense put a check on the imperialist intentions of direct aggression.

With the Revolution, Cuba not only obtained its true independence and recovered its national dignity, but also eliminated every form of exploitation and eradicated discrimination based on race and against women. To this may be added the social achievements and significant economic advances attained in the country.

The period of 1980 to 1985 was characterized by significant progress and achievements in economic and social development, despite the systematic increase in imperialist aggressiveness and adverse climatological phenomena. However, beginning in 1985, certain flaws and negative tendencies began to be evident, related mostly to the application of the management and planning system.

In April 1986, Fidel Castro, president of the councils of State and Ministers, spoke about the necessity of initiating a process of rectification of errors and negative tendencies that would provide a solution to the problems that were holding back and deforming the vital and original principles of the Cuban Revolution, such as constant popular population in discussions and tasks, unity between economic and social development, the creation of the «new man» that Che talked about, the return to historic values — principally, the ideas of Martí — and a more creative application of Marxism-Leninism. Despite defects and shortcomings, and the necessity of perfecting the work of socialist construction, the Cuban people had attained truly impressive achievements.

In health care, a comprehensive system was created that included everything from the family doctor and polyclinic to specialized hospitals and research centers. Free medical care is therefore part of a network that covers services for the entire population, from child care centers to schools to workplaces, and to the home.

In education, our country reports the best literacy rate in Latin America, with an average education of ninth grade. There is not a single child without a school.

Year after year, there are more professors, researchers, teachers, doctor and other university professionals.

With respect to sports, Cuba is among the ten top countries in the world.

Scientific and technical development deserves its own commentary, having become a vital factor in the survival of the country and the Revolution.

Institutions were founded such as the Center for Genetic and Biotechnological Engineering, the National Center of Scientific Research, the William Soler cardiac center for children's surgery (the largest in the world), the Immune Trials Center, and the Center for Transplants and Regeneration of the Nervous System.

An expression of this development is the creation of a magnetic resonance machine for imaging and thermographic analysis, and the Cuban laser scalpel.

Kidney, liver, heart and heart and lung transplants are performed in the country. In addition, important contributions to medicine have been made, such as the Cuban vaccine against meningococcal meningitis, human leukocyte alpha interferon, the discovery of a substance that cures vitiligo, and the obtaining of epidermal growth factor.

The Revolution was immersed in developing and perfecting this project when the socialist camp collapsed and the USSR disintegrated. These events were dramatically reflected in Cuban society, given that the country's economy was integrated into that community. That integration was even more determined by the severe, cruel and illegal blockade that the United States has maintained and continues to maintain against Cuba since the early years of the Revolution, and which moreover always placed an extraordinary limit on the possibility of relations with the capitalist world. In 1989, Cuba concentrated eighty-five percent of its trade relations with the USSR and the rest of the socialist camp. Fair prices were established for this trade, avoiding the unequal exchange typical of relations with developed capitalist countries. At the same time, it ensured the supply of technology and the granting of credit with satisfactory installment and interest terms.

When socialism collapsed in Europe and the USSR disintegrated, all in a very short amount of time, Cuba's buying capacity shrank from 8.139 million pesos in 1989 to 2.0 million in 1993.

The fall of socialism in Eastern Europe and in the USSR set off great euphoria in the U.S. government and among counterrevolutionary Cuban groups in Miami. It was predicted that the Cuban Revolution would fall apart in a matter of days or weeks. Political moves were even made for the organization and formation of a new government. However, the months passed and the crisis grew, but in Cuba there was no meltdown.

It should be said that since July of 1989, Commander in Chief Fidel Castro had warned of the possibility of the disappearance of socialist camp, and even about the disintegration of the USSR, and by October 1990, he had drawn up guidelines for facing the «Special Period in Peacetime.» This was a concept from the military doctrine of The War of the Entire People, and referred to measures for dealing with total blockade, air raids and systematic attrition, as well as a direct military invasion.

In 1991, the PCC held its Fourth Congress, analyzing the situation and stating explicitly the need to save the country, the Revolution and socialism, in other words, the project that had cost the Cuban people so much blood, sacrifice and effort over more than one hundred years of struggle. In this congress, important agreements were reached on changes to the Constitution and the Party's statutes, and the foundations were laid for a strategy for resisting and initiating recovery.

The strategy charted involved the implementation of a series of measures aimed at raising economic efficiency and competitiveness; an internal financial reorganization; solutions to internal indebtedness; reentry into the international economy; the encouragement of foreign capital investment, and the strengthening of Cuba's state enterprises, the last a necessary condition without which socialism is not possible. Discussion also centered on the need to increase and perfect any necessary economic changes in a gradual and orderly way.

As was to be expected, U.S. imperialism and unpatriotic groups in Miami, upset about the reality of Cuba's resistance, increased their actions to slander and destabilize the Revolution and further intensify the economic blockade.

Thus, in mid-1992, the U.S. government passed the Torricelli Law. Among other things, it gives the U.S. president the power to apply economic sanctions against countries that have trade relations with Cuba, and it prohibits trade with Cuba by subsidiaries of U.S. companies located in third countries. The law was yet another step in the attempt to bring the Cuban people to their knees through hunger.

However, despite the Torricelli Law, Cuba began expanding its trade and obtained some financing for certain economic activities and companies from several nations began to make investments and establish economic relations with Cuba.

Moreover, in February 1993, the most difficult year of the crisis, elections were held, and the outcome was irrefutable proof of popular support for the Revolution: 99.7 percent of voters cast their ballots, and only 7.3 percent cast blank or spoiled ballots.

Nevertheless, the anti-Cuban clique in the United States again resorted to trying to stir up internal subversion, terrorist acts, sabotage and the infiltration of CIA agents, and stepped up its anti-Cuba propaganda, including that directed at Cuba. More than 1,000 hours of radio time were targeted at the island. Priority was also given to encouraging illegal departures from the island, preferably by stealing boats or even airplanes.

The latter gave rise, in July of 1994, to the increased theft of boats by individuals chiefly under the pressure of the economic situation, although there were cases of murders. It was in these circumstances that a tugboat, the 13 de Marzo, was stolen and boarded by more than sixty people with the idea of traveling to the United States. Despite warnings about the boat's poor state, they began to flee, pursued by other tugboats, one of which crashed into the 13 de Marzo in an accident. All of the other vessels that arrived on the scene made enormous rescue efforts, but could not prevent thirty-two people from perishing. Based on this accident, a major campaign was waged, accusing the Cuban government of ordering the sinking of the tugboat.

In response to these events, the Cuban government decided not to prevent illegal departures, forcing the U.S. administration to sit at the negotiating table, and on September 9, 1994, to sign migratory accords with Cuba. After thirty-six years, the United States saw itself with the necessity of taking steps to discourage illegal departures to travel to that country.

In July 1995, the Cuban people once again gave a resounding show of unity and support for the Revolution when elections were held for People's Power delegates.

Despite the campaign of reactionary propaganda urging voters to abstain, 97.1 percent of voters cast their ballots, seven percent of ballots were annulled and 4.3 percent were blank. In other words, more than 87 percent of the electorate expressed their support for the Revolution.

After the mirage created by the collapse of the socialist camp, the frustrated counterrevolutionary clique of Cuban exiles and some groups within the U.S. government returned to the attack, this time with a Neanderthal-like project: the Helms-Burton Law.

This Law provided for a total, absolute and international blockade. It also attempted to block foreign investment and cut off all types of financing and supplies from outside Cuba. It established various penalties for companies or businesspeople who maintain economic relations with Cuba. In addition, it legalized U.S. support to counterrevolutionary groups on the island and established the right of the United States to determine what kind of government, society and relations Cuba should have after the Revolution's overthrow.

In short, it was an attempt to bring the Cuban people to their knees through hunger and to practically annex the island to the United States. After the law was passed by the U.S. Congress, extreme right-wing groups took advantage of an incident provoked by the Miami-based counterrevolutionary organization Brothers to the Rescue on February 24, 1996, when two planes were shot down after having violated Cuba's air space various times — which had led to warnings to the U.S. government — to pressure the U.S. administration to sign the law, which went into effect in August of that year.

It has not only aroused the rejection of the entire Cuban people, but also of almost all peoples and governments in the world, as well as international organizations and institutions. Evidence of that may be seen in votes against the blockade in the United Nations, the Organization of American States agreement opposing the Helms-Burton law, and the positions taken by Mexico, Canada, the European Union and the Rio Group, among others.

Despite the law's negative effects and its creation of a more complex and difficult situation, Cuba continued to implement its own strategy, and gradually, with serenity and determination, it was able to halt its economic decline and achieve a gradual revival in the following years.

In addition, its health, education, and social security systems were maintained. Not one Cuban was left abandoned; in 1997, the infant mortality rate was 7.3 per 1,000 live births, and the life expectancy rate was over 75 years.

In January 1998, elections were held for deputies to the National Assembly of People's Power and delegates to the provincial assemblies, and 98.35 percent of voters cast their ballots; 1.64 percent of the ballots were annulled and 3.36 percent were blank, for a total of 95 percent valid ballots. Of the valid ballots, 94.39 percent reflected a «united vote» for all of the candidates proposed by the National Electoral Commission.

That same month, Pope John Paul II visited Cuba. All of the people, believers and non-believers, provided a massive demonstration of hospitality and respect,  in his reception, at the masses he gave, and at all of the other activities. This showed the falsity of the propaganda campaigns spread by imperialism's apparatuses, because the whole world could see the freedom with which His Holiness acted and expressed himself at all times.

In conclusion, all of the imperialist and counterrevolutionary operations ignore something vital in our history: our people's capacity for resistance, the intelligence and skill of our revolutionary leadership, and the justness of this country's struggle for independence.

Flag of the Republic of Cuba

In 1850, what would end up being Cuba's national emblem was hoisted for the first time. With great simplicity and in perfect harmony, three colors are combined: red, blue and white, to form the Cuban flag. Its beautiful design is comprised of three red stripes, the three departments into which the island was divided at the time; two white stripes, the strength of the independence ideal; a red triangle, representing equality, fraternity and liberty, and at the same time, the blood necessarily spilled in the independence struggles; and a white, solitary star, as a symbol of the absolute freedom among the rest of the peoples.

The national coat of arms represents our island. It is shaped like an ogival leather shield and is divided into three fields.

Its horizontal upper field features a golden key between two mountains and a rising sun over the sea, which symbolizes Cuba's position in the Gulf between the two Americas, in the midst of the emergence of a new state. The white and blue bands stand for the island's position as a department in colonial times, and occupy the entire left field. In the right field: a Cuban landscape presided over by the Royal Palm, the symbol of the undefeatable character of the Cuban people.

National Anthem

The Cuban national anthem was born in Bayamo, in the heat of the struggle for independence. After having composed the melody in 1867, Pedro Figueredo, with a great, pro-independence spirit, wrote the lyrics of this battle hymn when the revolutionary troops occupied the city in 1868.

Hasten to battle, men of Bayamo!
The fatherland looks proudly to you;
Do not fear a glorious death,
Because to die for the fatherland is to live.

To live in chains is to live
In dishonour and ignominy,
Hear the clarion's call;
Hasten, brave ones, to battle!

Cuba. Division by provinces

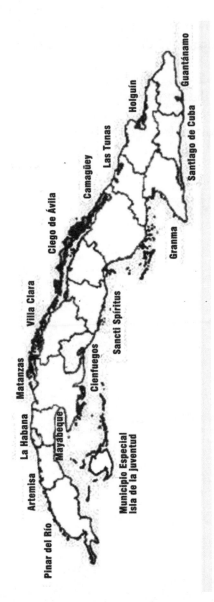

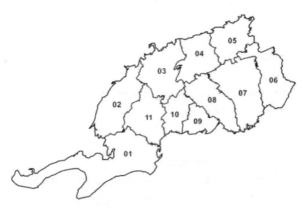

Municipalities
01 Sandino
02 Mantua
03 Minas de Matahambre
04 Viñales
05 La Palma
06 Los Palacios
07 Consolación del Sur
08 Pinar del Río
09 San Luis
10 San Juan y Martínez
11 Guane

Geographical location: western region, between latitude 21°19' and 22° 56' North and between longitude 84°57' abd 83° 05' West.

It is the fourth largest province, with 8 ,84.51 square kilometers and the eighth in population density with 592,851 inhabitants.

Geographical boundaries:
To the north: Gulf of Mexico
To the east: Artemisa province
To the south: Caribbean Sea
To the west: Yucatan Canal

Longest river: Cuyaguateje
Highest peak: Loma de Seboruco, 671 meters high.

Physical geography:

The landscape is characterized by the Guaniguanico mountain range, highlighting the Sierra de los Órganos, which is located entirely in the territory, What is added to a small part of the Sierra del Rosario, where is the highest elevation in the province. These bordering them the plains of the North and South of Pinar del Río, Guanahacabibes and Guane-Mantua. Its hydrographic features include short, shallow rivers, with the exception of Cuyaguateje, Hondo, Ajiconal and San Diego; a large number of lakes, such as the Santa María and El Pesquero. Its main reservoirs are the Juventud and El Punto. Hydromorphic soils predominate in the lower coastal areas, while a combination of ferralitic, grey-brown and little-evolved soils do in the rest of the province.

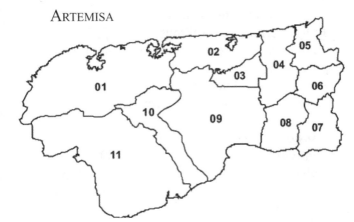

Municipalities
01 Bahía Honda
02 Mariel
03 Guanajay
04 Caimito
05 Bauta
06 San Antonio de los Baños
07 Güira de Melena
08 Alquizar
09 Artemisa
10 Candelaria
11 San Cristobal

Geographical location: western region, between latitude 22° 29' and 23° 05' North and between longitude 83 °25' and 82° 28' West.

It is the tenth largest province, with 4,004.27 square kilometers, and the eleventh in population density with 502,312 inhabitants.

Geographical boundaries:
To the north: Florida Straits
To the east:: La Habana and Mayabeque provinces
To the south: Gulf of Batabanó
To the west: Pinar del Río province

Longest river: Los Colorados
Highest peak: Pan de Guajaibón, 692 meters high.

Physical geography:
Dominated by the topography of plains, highlighting the Havana-Matanzas plain. It includes the western part of the plain South Habana-Matanzas, the heights of Mariel and the Anafe table. The Sierra del Rosario in the Guaniguanico Cordillera, where is the highest elevation in the province. Its hydrography is characterized by short rivers and little flow, highlighting Los Colorados River and San Juan. Dominate the soils fersialitics, Brown, ferralitics, hydromorphologic and humic calcimorfics.

HAVANA

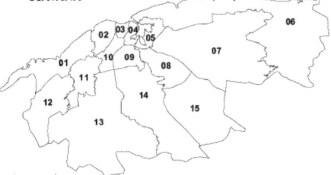

Municipalities
01 Playa
02 Plaza de la Revolución
03 Centro Habana
04 La Habana Vieja
05 Regla
06 La Habana del Este
07 Guanabacoa
08 San Miguel del Padrón
09 Diez de Octubre
10 Cerro
11 Marianao
12 La Lisa
13 Boyeros
14 Arroyo Naranjo
15 Cotorro

Geographical location: western region, between latitude 22° 58' and 23° 10' North and between longitude 82°30' and 82° 06' West.

It is the sixteenth largest province, with 726.75 square kilometers, and the firsth in population density with 2,141,652 inhabitants.

Geographical boundaries:
To the north: Florida Straits
To the east: Mayabeque province
To the south: Mayabeque and Artemisa provinces
To the west: Artemisa province

Longest river: Almendares
Highest peak: Tetas de Managua, 210 meters high.

Physical geography:
Its territory is occupied by the La Habana-Matanzas plains and heights. The coasts occupy the entire northern boundary, where Havana bay is located, and beaches are to the east. Hydrographic features include the rivers Almendares, Martín Pérez, and Quibú, among others, and the reservoirs Bacuranao and Ejército Rebelde. Non-urbanized, fersialitic, reddish-grey and red ferralitic soils predominate, while in some coastal areas, bare carsic rock can be seen.

Mayabeque

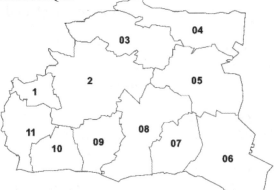

Municipalities
01 Bejucal
02 San José de las Lajas
03 Jaruco
04 Santa Cruz del Norte
05 Madruga
06 Nueva Paz
07 San Nicolás
08 Güines
09 Melena del Sur
10 Batabanó
11 Quivicán

Geographical location: western region, between latitude 22°34' and 23° 12' North and between longitude 82°28' and 81° 40' West.

It is the tenth largest province, with 3,732.73 square kilometers, and the fifteenth in population density with 381,385 inhabitants.

Geographical boundaries:
To the north: La Habana province and Florida Straits
To the east: Matanzas province
To the south: Gulf of Batabanó
To the west: Artemisa province

Longest river: Mayabeque
Highest peak: El Palenque, 332 meters high.

Physical geography:

Its terrain is characterized by the plain Havana-Matanzas where the plain South Havana-Matanzas and the heights of Bejucal and Madruga, belonging to the heights Bejucal-Madruga-Coliseum, where is the highest elevation in the province. The rivers are short and little flow, highlighting the Mayabeque, Canasí and Jibacoa, rivers dominate soils fersialitics, Brown, ferralitics and humic calcimorfics.

Municipalities
01 Matanzas
02 Cárdenas
03 Martí
04 Colón
05 Perico
06 Jovellanos
07 Pedro Betancourt
08 Limonar
09 Unión de Reyes
10 Ciénaga de Zapata
11 Jagüey Grande
12 Calimete
13 Los Arabos

Geographical location: western region, between latitude 24°01' and 23°15' North and between longitude 80°31' and 82°09' West.

It is the second largest province, with 11,798.02 square kilometers, and the seventh in population density with 690,113 inhabitants.

Geographical boundaries:
To the north: Florida Straits
To the east: Villa Clara and Cienfuegos provinces
To the south: Caribbean sea
To the west: Mayabeque province and Broa Cove

Longest river: La Palma
Highest peak: Pan de Matanzas, 381 meters high.

Physical geography:
The plains predominate, occupying 80 percent of the total area, with heights in the northwest and central west areas of the La Habana-Matanzas heights, and with the Pan de Matanzas as the highest peak. Principle hydric reserves are in the aquifer, while the most important fluvial currents are the rivers Hanábana, Canímar and Yumurí, along with major bays. Its soils are fertile and productive, allocated for agricultural activities; especially notable are its red ferralitic soils, with small areas of calcimorphic humic and hydromorphic marshy soils.

CIENFUEGOS

Municipalities
01 Aguada de Pasajeros
02 Rodas
03 Palmira
04 Lajas
05 Cruces
06 Cumanayagua
07 Cienfuegos
08 Abreus

Geographical location: located in the south of the central region, between latitude 21°50' and 22°30' North and between longitude 80°06' and 80°55' West.

It is the twelfth largest province, with 4,186.60 square kilometers, and the fourteenth in population density with 405,481 inhabitants.

Geographical boundaries:
To the north: Villa Clara and Matanzas provinces

To the east: Villa Clara and Sancti Spíritus provinces
To the south: Caribbean sea
To the west: Matanzas province

Longest river: Hanábana
Highest peak: Pico San Juan, 1,140 meters high.

Physical geography:
The Cienfuegos and Manacas plains prevail; to the east, the Santa Clara heights and the Guamuhaya Mountains; the Cave of Martín Infierno is located here, with a stalagmite 50 meters high and 30 meters in diameter, and the province contains a number of deposits for construction materials. Its hydrographic features include the rivers Hanábana, Caunao, and Arimao, among others, and the mineral/medicinal and thermal waters of Ciego Montero. The bay of Cienfuegos stands out for its depth, narrow channel and broad interior. Grey soils predominate, with and without carbonates, as well as red ferralitic and typical humic soils.

Villa Clara

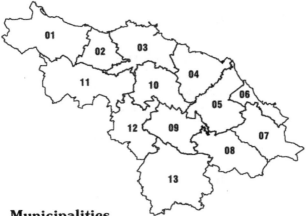

Municipalities

01 Corralillo
02 Quemado de Güines
03 Sagua la Grande
04 Encrucijada
05 Camajuaní
06 Caibarién
07 Remedios
08 Placetas
09 Santa Clara
10 Cifuentes
11 Santo Domingo
12 Ranchuelo
13 Manicaragua

Geographical location: located in the central region, between latitude 22°16' and 23°09' North and between longitude 80°02' and 80°25' West.

It is the fifth largest province, with 8,413.13 square kilometers, and the fifth in population density with 803,562 inhabitants.

Geographical boundaries:
To the north: Atlantic Ocean
To the east: Sancti Spíritus province
To the south: Sancti Spíritus province
To the west: Matanzas and Cienfuegos provinces

Longest river: Sagua la Grande
Highest peak: Pico Tuerto, 919 meters high.

Physical geography:
The landscape is characterized by the central heights of northern Cuba, the Manacas plains and the Santa Clara heights. Its hydrographic features include the rivers Sagua la Grande and Sagua la Chica and the Alacranes Reservoir. Dark, plastic, non-gleyed soils and brown carbonated and red ferralitic soils predominate.

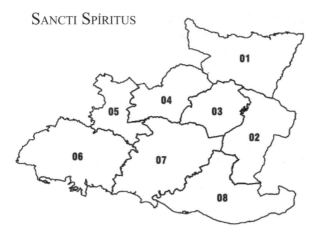

Municipalities
01 Yaguajay
02 Jatibonico
03 Taguasco
04 Cabaiguán
05 Fomento
06 Trinidad
07 Sancti Spíritus
08 La Sierpe

Geographical location: located in the central region, between latitude 21°32' and 22°27' North and between longitude 78°56' and 80°07' West.

It is the eighth largest province, with 6,779.81 square kilometers, and the twelfth in population density with 465,468 inhabitants.

Geographical boundaries:
To the north: Old Bahamas Channel
To the east: Ciego de Ávila province
To the south: Caribbean Sea
To the west: Cienfuegos and Villa Clara provinces

Longest river: Zaza
Highest peak: Pico Potrerillo, 931 meters high.

Physical geography:
   The landscape is very diverse. In the north, there is a narrow strip of the northern plains of central Cuba, there are the Bamburanao and Meneses-Cueto mountain ranges, and more towards the center stand the Fomento hills and the Guamuhaya Mountains. Hydrographical features include long rivers, and particularly noteworthy are the River Jatibonico del Norte, Higuanojo, Yayabo, Jatibonico del Sur and Zaza. Brown, carbonated and non-carbonated soils prevail, and elsewhere, typical red ferralitic and hydromorphic soils.

Ciego de Ávila

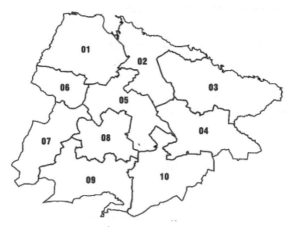

Municipalities

01 Chambas
02 Morón
03 Bolivia
04 Primero de Enero
05 Ciro Redondo
06 Florencia
07 Majagua
08 Ciego de Ávila
09 Venezuela
10 Baraguá

Geographical location: located east of the central region, between latitude 20°50' and 22°41' North and between longitude 78°04' and 79°08' West.

It is the seventh largest province, with 6,946,.90 square kilometers, and the thirteenth in population density with 422,576 inhabitants.

Geographical boundaries:
To the north: Old Bahamas Channel
To the east: Camagüey province
To the south: Gulf of Ana María
To the west: Sancti Spíritus province

Longest river: Majagua
Highest peak: Sierra de Jatibonico, 443 meters high.

Physical geography:
Carsic plains predominate with isolated elevations, and features include the plains of Sancti Spíritus, in the northern part of central Cuba, the Sierra de Jatibonico mountains and the Tamarindo hills. Hydrographic features include its small, shallow rivers, with the largest being the Chambas, Calvario, Majagua and Itabo; the largest reservoirs are the Chambas Uno and the Chambas Dos. Very productive ferralitic soils prevail, with hydromorphic soils in the plains and lower areas, and grey soils in the higher altitudes.

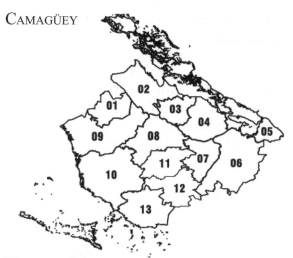

Municipalities

01 Carlos M. de Céspedes
02 Esmeralda
03 Sierra de Cubitas
04 Minas
05 Nuevitas
06 Guáimaro
07 Sibanicú
08 Camagüey
09 Florida
10 Vertientes
11 Jimaguayú
12 Najasa
13 Santa Cruz del Sur

Geographical location: located east of the central region, between latitude 20°27' and 22°29' North and between longitude 78°00' and 78°10' West.

It is the largest province, with 15,413.82 square kilometers, and the sixth in population density with 782,458 inhabitants.

Geographical boundaries:
To the north: Old Bahamas Channel
To the east: Las Tunas province
To the south: Caribbean Sea
To the west: Ciego de Ávila province

Longest river: Caonao
Highest peak: Cerro Tuabaquey, 330 meters high.

Physical geography:
High, medium and low plains predominate; from the north, center and south of Camagüey-Las Tunas. Hydrographical features include the rivers Caonao, San Pedro, Máximo and Saramaguacán and the reservoirs Jimaguayú, Porvenir, Amistad Cubano-Búlgara and Muñoz. Grey carbonated, calcimorphic humic, fersialitic, hydromorphic and vertisol soils predominate.

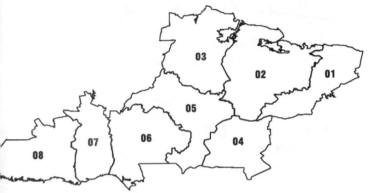

Municipalities
01 Manatí
02 Puerto Padre
03 Jesús Menéndez
04 Majibacoa
05 Las Tunas
06 Jobabo
07 Colombia
08 Amancio

Geographical location: located in the eastern region, between latitude 20°30' and 21°27' North and between longitude 77°48' and 76°58' West.

It is the ninth largest province, with 6,595.25 square kilometers, and the ninth in population density with 536,027 inhabitants.

Geographical boundaries:
To the north: Camagüey province and the Atlantic Ocean
To the east: Holguín province
To the south: Granma province and the Gulf of Guacanayabo
To the west: Camagüey province

Longest river: Tana
Highest peak: Alturas de Cañada Honda, 219 meters high.

Physical geography:
The plains predominate; to the north, the Northern Camagüey-Las Tunas plains, where the hills of Caisimú, Dumañuecos, Cerro Verde, and loma Jengibre are located, the Southern Camagüey-Las Tunas plains and the Cauto plains. Its hydrographic features include the rivers Chaparra, Jobabo, Sevilla, El Tana and the reservoirs Juan Sáez, Las Mercedes, Gramal, Ciego and Yariguá. Grey, ferralitic, hydromorphic and vertisol soils predominate.

Municipalities

01 Río Cauto
02 Cauto Cristo
03 Jiguaní
04 Bayamo
05 Yara
06 Manzanillo
07 Campechuela
08 Media Luna
09 Niquero
10 Pilón
11 Bartolomé Masó
12 Buey Arriba
13 Guisa

Geographical location: located southwest of the eastern region, between latitude 19°50' and 20°39' North and between longitude 76°22' and 77°44' West.

It is the sixth largest province, with 8,376.79 square kilometers, and the fourth in population density with 835,675 inhabitants.

Geographical boundaries:
To the north: Las Tunas and Holguín provinces
To the east: Holguín and Santiago de Cuba provinces
To the south: Santiago de Cuba province and the Caribbean Sea
To the west: Gulf of Guacanayabo

Longest river: Cauto
Highest peak: Pico Bayamesa, 1,756 meters high.

Physical geography:
The Cauto plains and the Sierra Maestra orographic groups, including the Bayamesa and Martí peaks. Its hydrographic features include the rivers Cauto, Limones, Gua, Yara, and Hicotea, and the reservoirs Cauto del Paso, Paso Malo, Pedregales, and Buey; its largest lakes are the Birama, Carenas, and Las Playas, among others. Hydromorphic, vertisol, and calcimorphic humic soils predominated in the planes, and grey soils at higher altitudes.

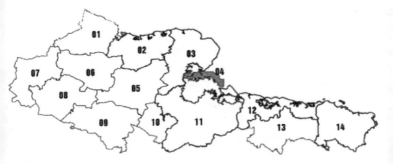

Municipalities
01 Gibara
02 Rafael Freyre
03 Banes
04 Antilla
05 Báguano
06 Holguín
07 Calixto García
08 Cacocum
09 Urbano Noris
10 Cueto
11 Mayarí
12 Frank País
13 Sagua de Tánamo
14 Moa

Geographical location: ocated northwest of the eastern region, between latitude 21°15' and 20°24' North and between longitude 76°19' and 74°50' West.

It is the third largest province, with 9,209.71 square kilometers, and the third in population density with 1,037,161 inhabitants.

Geographical boundaries:
To the north: Atlantic Ocean
To the east: Guantánamo province
To the south: Santiago de Cuba and Granma provinces
To the west: Las Tunas province

Longest river: Mayarí
Highest peak: Pico Cristal, 1,231 meters high.

Physical geography:
Dominant features are the Maniabón heights, the Cauto plains, the Nipe plains and the Nipe-Sagua-Baracoa Mountains. Its hydrographic features include the rivers Mayarí, Gibara, Sagua de Tánamo, and Tacajó and the reservoirs Gibara, Cacoyugüin, and Sabanilla, and the bays of Gibara, Banes, and Nipe. Ferromagnesian soil grayish-red soils, reddish-grey fersialitic soils and gleyed plastic dark soils predominate.

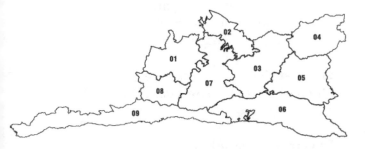

Municipalities
01 Contramaestre
02 Mella
03 San Luis
04 Segundo Frente
05 Songo–La Maya
06 Santiago de Cuba
07 Palma Soriano
08 Tercer Frente
09 Guamá

Geographical location: Located south of the eastern region, between latitude 19°53' and 20°12' North and between longitude 75°22' and 77°02' West.

It is the tenth largest province, with 6,234.16 square kilometers, and the second in population density with 1,047,015 inhabitants.

Geographical boundaries:

To the north: Holguín province
To the east: Guantánamo province
To the south: Caribbean Sea
To the west: Granma province

Longest river: Contramaestre
Highest peak: Pico Real del Turquino, 1,974 meters high.

Physical geography:

Almost the entire province is mountainous, occupied by the Sierra Maestra and the southern slopes of the Nipe Mountains and the Cristal, and flat in the eastern tip of the Cauto plains, the Santiago de Cuban basin and the Valle Central. Hydrographic features include the rivers Contramaestre, Guaninicum and Baconao; the reservoirs Protesta de Baraguá and Carlos Manuel de Céspedes and Lake Baconao. Grey, non-carbonated soils and yellowish fersialitic soils predominate.

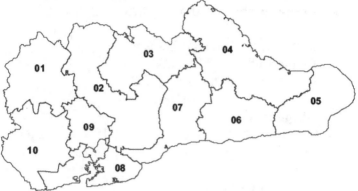

Municipalities
01 El Salvador
02 Manuel Tames
03 Yateras
04 Baracoa
05 Maisí
06 Imías
07 San Antonio del Sur
08 Caimanera
09 Guantánamo
10 Niceto Pérez

Geographical location: Located in the eastern region, between latitude 19°54' and 20°30' North and between longitude 74°08' and 75°30' West.

It is the eleventh largest province, with 6,164.47 square kilometers, and the tenth in population density with 510,863 inhabitants.

Geographical boundaries:
To the north: Holguín province and Atlantic Ocean
To the east: Windward Passage
To the south: Caribbean Sea
To the west: Santiago de Cuba province

Longest river: Toa
Highest peak: Pico El Gato, 1,184 meters high.

Physical geography:
The landscape is dominated by elevations: the Nipe-Sagua-Baracoa Mountains, part of the Sierra Maestra, the valleys of Guantánamo, Central, and Caujerí and plains with typical marine terraces. Its hydrographical features include the rivers Toa, Duaba, Yumurí, Guantánamo, Guaso and Sabanalamar. Its main lake is La Salada and its largest reservoirs are the Yaya and the Jaibo. Grey carbonated, fersialitic and hydromorphic soils predominate in the lower, marshy areas, and there are salt deposits.

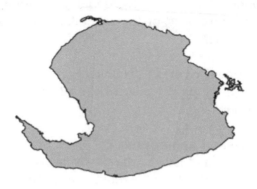

Because of its surface area, population and economic characteristics, this is considered as a special municipality, and is not attached to any province.

Ubicación geográfica: located in the Gulf of Batabanó and north of the Caribbean Sea, in the western region, at latitude 21°42' North and longitude 82°50' West.

Its surface area covers 2,419.27 square kilometers, representing 2.2 percent of the country's total surface area.

Geographical boundaries:
To the north: Waters of the Gulf of Batabanó
To the east: Water platform ínsular and Matanzas province
To the south: Caribbean Sea
To the west: Water platform ínsular and Pinar del Río province

107

It represents 0.8 percent of the country's population, with 86,242 inhabitants, for a population density of 35.6 inhabitants per square kilometer.

Longest river: Las Nuevas
Highest peak: Sierra de La Cañada, 303 meters high.

Physical geography:
The land is flat, with plains in the north of the island, where the mountain ranges Casas, Caballos and La Cañada are located; and plains in the southern part of the island. Its hydrographic features include the rivers Las Nuevas, San Pedro, Las Casas, and Júcaro, and its reservoirs include the Viet-Nam Heroico. Hydromorphic soils predominate on the coasts, while in the central region, they are ferralitic, and in the south, calcimorphic humic.